Pronunciation Workouts

PronPack 1
Pronunciation Workouts

- A four-book set for teachers of English
- Fun-packed pronunciation activities
- Easy-to-follow presentation notes
- Extra resources on PronPack.com
- Print-friendly worksheets

By Mark Hancock

Hancock McDonald
ENGLISH LANGUAGE TEACHING

PronPack 1
Pronunciation Workouts

By Mark Hancock

Published by **Hancock McDonald ELT**
Chester. CH1 2AW UK
www.hancockmcdonald.com

First Published 2017

ISBN: 978-0-9957575-1-6

Contents

End Matter

Introduction

The Book

What is PronPack?

PronPack is a set of four resource books to help teachers focus on English pronunciation in class. The books contain printable worksheets along with teacher's notes explaining how to use them. Each of the four books takes a slightly different approach to pronunciation teaching. You can select the approach you prefer, or use the various books to complement one another.

What are Pronunciation Workouts?

Pronunciation Workouts are extended drills focusing on specific areas of English pronunciation. Think of them like the scales and other exercises pianists use to improve their fingering technique, or like a fitness workout which a gymnast might use to tone the muscles. In the case of pronunciation, it's the vocal articulators which are being trained – the tongue, lips, jaw and vocal chords.

What are the benefits of doing these workouts?

The workouts can benefit learners in two different ways – practice and perception.

Practice: The workouts can help the mouth muscles to become accustomed to the unfamiliar movements required to speak in English. New skills are often very difficult at first, but with practice, we gradually get used to them. Think of driving, for example.

Perception: The workouts help learners to notice features of English pronunciation: the target pronunciation feature is repeated so often in the workout, that it becomes much more obvious. The learner becomes familiar with how it sounds and how it feels to articulate it. To return to the music metaphor, playing exercises on the piano helps the learner develop an intuitive sense of how the notes sound relative to one another, and how the fingers feel while playing them on the keyboard.

What aspects of pronunciation are covered in PronPack 1?

The earlier workouts in the book focus on the sound system of English. These serve to familiarize the learners with the system as a whole by exploring the **PronPack Sound Chart**. They focus on different regions of the system, such as the short vowels or the stop consonants, and they help the learner become more aware of the articulators in the mouth and vocal tract. The later workouts in the book focus on suprasegmental features such as word stress, connected speech and tonic stress.

What are the other books in the PronPack collection?

The other three books in the series are:

PronPack 2: Pronunciation Puzzles – puzzles and game-like activities.
PronPack 3: Pronunciation Pairworks – communication activities.
PronPack 4: Pronunciation Poems – poems, raps and chants.

The Approach

Why teach pronunciation?

The most important reason to teach pronunciation is to help your students understand and be understood. As listeners, they need to learn how other speakers blend sounds into words and words into connected speech. As speakers, they need to modify their own accent of English to make it as widely intelligible as possible. Neither of these objectives requires them to precisely copy the accent of a native speaker. The aim is successful communication, not 'correctness'.

What is the pronunciation model?

In the context of your classroom, the best pronunciation model is almost certainly you, the teacher. PronPack aims to be as flexible as possible – you should be able to work with it whether your own accent is from London or Sydney, Turkey or Argentina. Although the phonemic symbols used are based on a British model, they are not intended to be prescriptive. For instance, /e/ does not specify the precise quality of the vowel, but merely that it is different from /æ/ or /ɪ/.

Do I have to know the phonemic alphabet?

You don't necessarily have to know or use the phonemic alphabet. There is a version of the **PronPack Sound Chart** which uses normal alphabet spellings. Where the phonemic symbols are used in other workouts, they are always accompanied by a guide word so the students do not need to know the symbols beforehand.

Do these activities work only for one accent?

The material does not restrict you to teaching towards a specific accent. For instance, the activities don't prescribe the **silent r** in words like *hair*, *arm*, *fork* and *bird*. It is optional, and is shown in brackets in the **PronPack Sound Chart**. If you choose to model the workouts yourself and you have an accent where the **silent r** is pronounced, the activities still work fine. However, the audio files, if you choose to use them, are recorded in a General British accent. Note that there is both a British and an American version of the **PronPack Sound Chart**.

Note that the symbols which appear between slanted brackets in this book, such as /ʌ/ or /ʃ/, are strictly speaking, phonemes rather than sounds. A phoneme such as /ʌ/ corresponds to slightly different sounds across different accents.

Flexi notes throughout the books highlight ways that you can adapt the material to work with different accents.

The Activities

What materials are in the book?

The book contains printable worksheets for the students and teacher's notes for you. The teacher's notes highlight the teaching focus, minimum student level, and indicate printing requirements and audio files available for each activity. The notes give a short background to the pronunciation point plus a step-by-step procedure for using the activity in class.

How long do the activities take?

Each activity will typically take around 15-20 minutes of class time, although this can vary a lot depending on how thoroughly you exploit the material. If you would like to spend longer, you can combine the *workout* activity with a *puzzle*, *pairwork* or *poem* focusing on the same pronunciation point from **PronPack 2**, **3** or **4**. Recommended combinations are given in the *Lesson Plans* section, page 10 and in the **Goes well with ...** notes at the end of each activity.

Do I have to print out the worksheets?

The worksheets in ***Pronunciation Workouts*** may be printed and/or projected. They are particularly good when projected because this enables you to point and direct attention to specific parts of the worksheet. None of the activities in this book require the students to write or draw on the worksheet, with the exception of activity **1.2**.

What level are the activities designed for?

The minimum level is indicated in the teacher's notes for each workout, but remember that this is a minimum level. An activity which is suitable for a pre-intermediate learner can be just as valuable for an upper intermediate learner – pronunciation often lags behind other competences because it has been neglected.

Are the activities for a specific age group or class size?

The activities are not aimed at a specific age group and should benefit young learners and adults alike. The workouts in this book function in any size of class, but most of them are choral chants and will lose a lot of their appeal if there are only two or three students in the room.

What are the audio files for?

Apart from the book itself, there are audio files for most of the lessons. Teachers can use these if they are not confident about their own pronunciation. However, you can model the workouts yourself instead of using the audio files, and this is usually the better option. If you do this, it is wise to practise saying them a couple of times before class so that you know where difficulties might lie for your students. You could use the audio to guide you in this rehearsal.

The Website

What will I find on the support website?

PronPack.com provides additional information for users of *PronPack* including downloadable poster versions of the *PronPack Sound Charts* and Free extra pronunciation activities.

If you have purchased an ePub or the print-version of this book we would like to thank you for supporting our endeavour. On the website you will have access to teacher resources to accompany the activities including:

- Print-friendly PDF files of the activity worksheets

- Slides to use during the presentation phase of the lessons

- Downloadable MP3 audio files as required

- Updates and additional materials

Note: The interactive functionality of the fixed-layout ePub will depend on your device and/or the ePub reader available for your device.

Contact us

We'd welcome your feedback on www.pronpack.com and invite you to share your thoughts and reactions on the book seller's website.

Please get in touch with us through our website if you have any difficulties with the material or would like to make a suggestion for another activity.

Connect with us on:

 twitter.com/pronpackbooks (@pronpackbooks)

 facebook.com/pronpack

Lesson Plans

If you plan to focus on a particular pronunciation point, here are some recommended activity combinations from across the complete **PronPack Collection** (Books **1**, **2**, **3** and **4**):

- **Awareness of sounds: 2.1, 2.6**
- **The complete sound system: 1.1, 1.2, 1.3**
- **Long versus short vowels: 3.1** Version 1, **3.2** Version 2, **4.1**
- **The R vowels: 1.4, 2.2** Version 4, **4.3**
- **Vowels spelt with 2 letters: 1.5, 2.12, 2.2** Version 5, **4.4**
- **Short vowels: 1.6, 2.3, 3.1** Version 2, **3.3** vowel pairs, **4.2**
- **Stop consonants: 1.7, 3.4** Version 1, **3.3** consonant pairs, **4.11**
- **Fricatives and affricates: 1.8, 2.2** Version 2, **3.4** Version 3, **4.9, 4.10**
- **Semi-vowels: 2.2** Version 3, **3.4** Version 2, **4.7**
- **/l/ versus /r/: 3.2** Version 3, **3.5** Version 3, **4.8**
- **Consonant clusters: 1.9 , 4.13**
- **-ed endings: 2.2** Version 6, **4.14**
- **/s/ versus /z/ and –s endings: 2.2** Version 1, **3.5** Version 2, **4.15**
- **Word stress: 2.9, 3.6**
- **Word stress families: 1.10, 2.7, 3.8, 4.16**
- **Weak forms: 1.11, 2.4** Version 2, **4.5, 4.17**
- **Rhythm: 1.12, 4.16**
- **Tonic stress: 1.13, 2.9, 3.10, 3.11, 3.12**
- **Connected speech: 2.5, 2.10, 3.9**

Goes well with ...

... These combinations are also given at the end of each activity.

Map of the book

The PronPack Sound Chart	A teaching and reference tool for the individual sounds of English, including an explanatory infographic. There are six versions of the Chart: **IPA**; **Typical spellings**; and **American** – each has a version with guidewords and a version with pictures.			
WORKOUTS	**TEACHING FOCUS**	**MINIMUM LEVEL**	**ACTIVITY**	
1.1 **Presenting the PronPack Sound Chart**	The sound system of English	Elementary upwards	Exploring the sound system of English	
1.2 **Vowel Chart Pathfinder**	The vowel sound chart; fostering learner autonomy	Pre-intermediate	Listen and follow a route	
1.3 **Tongue Cats**	The role of tongue, jaw and lips in vowel sounds	Pre-intermediate	Articulation workout; lip reading	
1.4 **R-Vowel Workout**	R-vowel articulation and sound-spelling patterns	Pre-intermediate	Articulation workout; spelling pattern spotting	
1.5 **Alphabet Vowel Workout**	Alphabet vowel articulation and sound-spelling patterns	Pre-intermediate	Articulation workout; spelling pattern spotting	
1.6 **Short Vowel Workout**	Short vowel distinctions and sound-spelling patterns	Pre-intermediate	Articulation workout; spelling pattern spotting	
1.7 **Stop Consonant Workout**	The stop consonants and nasals	Pre-intermediate	Exploring the stops and nasals; a minimal pair activity	
1.8 **Friction Consonant Workout**	The fricative consonants	Pre-intermediate	Exploring the fricatives; a minimal pair activity	
1.9 **Cluster Clocks**	Syllable structure and practise of consonant clusters	Pre-intermediate	Choral chant/drill	
1.10 **Word Stress Workout**	Word stress	Intermediate	Choral chant/drill	
1.11 **Bricks and Mortar**	Weak forms and connected speech	Pre-intermediate to Intermediate	Choral chant/drill	
1.12 **Rhythm Workout**	Rhythm	Pre-intermediate	Choral chant/drill	
1.13 **Tonic Stress Workout**	Tonic stress	Pre-intermediate	Choral chant/drill	

The PronPack Sound Chart

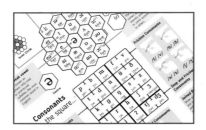

PRONPACK SOUND CHARTS

PronPack Infographic

PronPack Sound Chart 1

PronPack Sound Chart 2

PronPack Sound Chart 3

PronPack Sound Chart 4

PronPack Sound Chart 5

PronPack Sound Chart 6

What is the Sound Chart for?

Reference

The **PronPack Sound Chart** is primarily a reference tool. Teachers may print a copy as large as possible to put on the classroom wall. Whenever a pronunciation point comes up in class relating to one or more of the individual sounds, you can point it out on the chart.

Over time, the class will become more and more familiar with it. However, to get students started with the chart, you may want to devote some class time to presenting and exploring it more intensively. You can use lessons **1.1 PronPack Sound Chart Guided Tour** and **1.2 Vowel Chart Pathfinder** in this book for this purpose.

Orientation

The **PronPack Sound Chart** is intended to help you and the class find your way around the sounds of English. It enables you to see the 'big picture' – the entire system – at a glance. This is useful because if you just encounter the sounds one by one, you have no idea of where you are in the system as a whole. It could appear limitless and consequently impossible to master.

Comparison

The **PronPack Sound Chart** graphically represents relationships between the sounds, showing those that are comparable with one another and those which are very different. This helps to promote an understanding of the whole system, as well as making it more memorable. Regular users will eventually be able to remember which sound occupies which place in the chart as a whole.

How is the Sound Chart organised?

The **PronPack Sound Chart Infogaphic** on page 13 explains how the Sound Chart is organised. This is primarily for you, but you could print it out for your students at the beginning of the course too.

Note: You will find downloadable poster versions of the **PronPack Sound Charts** at **www.pronpack.com**

Vowels
in the hexagon...

Six Short vowels
Symbols are all single; these vowels never end a syllable.

Inner Circle

Six Long vowels
Symbols usually have : but /eə/ also considered a long vowel in this model.

Outer Circle

Corners

Six Diphthongs
Symbols have two elements; the sound moves from one position to the other.

Sides

The weak vowel
Also known as 'schwa'; only used in unstressed syllables; the most common sound in English!

Jaw and lip positions

closed - wide | closed - round
mid - wide | relaxed
open - wide | open - round

Optional r
The letter **r** usually comes after these sounds; pronounced in some accents, not in others.

Centre

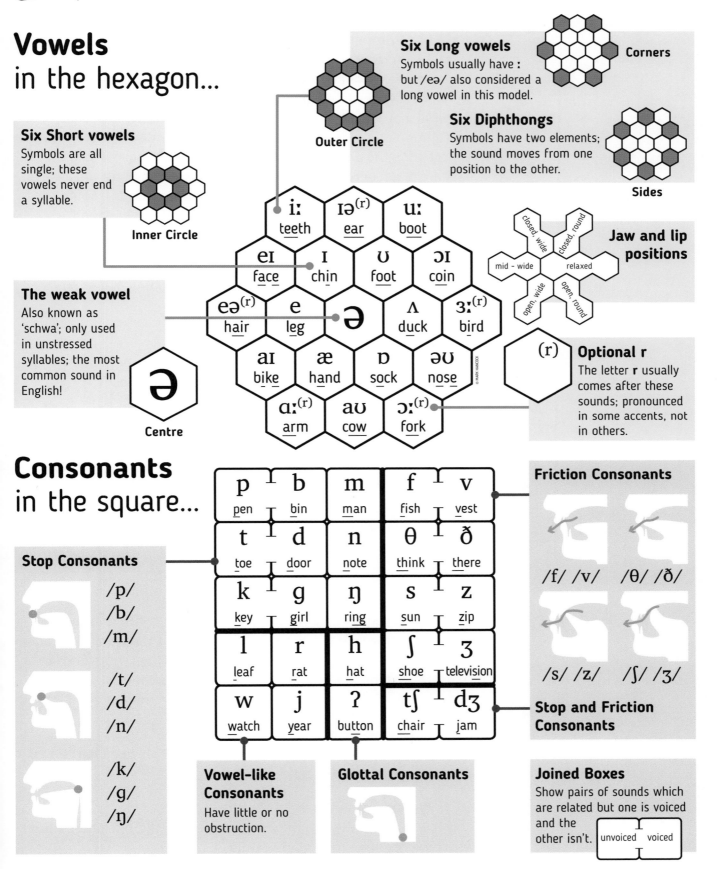

Hexagon vowels:
iː teeth · ɪə⁽ʳ⁾ ear · uː boot · eɪ face · ɪ chin · ʊ foot · ɔɪ coin · eə⁽ʳ⁾ hair · e leg · ə · ʌ duck · ɜː⁽ʳ⁾ bird · aɪ bike · æ hand · ɒ sock · əʊ nose · ɑː⁽ʳ⁾ arm · aʊ cow · ɔː⁽ʳ⁾ fork

© MARK HANCOCK

Consonants
in the square...

Stop Consonants

/p/
/b/
/m/

/t/
/d/
/n/

/k/
/g/
/ŋ/

Consonant square:
p pen	b bin	m man	f fish	v vest
t toe	d door	n note	θ think	ð there
k key	g girl	ŋ ring	s sun	z zip
l leaf	r rat	h hat	ʃ shoe	ʒ television
w watch	j year	ʔ button	tʃ chair	dʒ jam

Friction Consonants

/f/ /v/   /θ/ /ð/

/s/ /z/   /ʃ/ /ʒ/

Stop and Friction Consonants

Vowel-like Consonants
Have little or no obstruction.

Glottal Consonants

Joined Boxes
Show pairs of sounds which are related but one is voiced and the other isn't.
unvoiced | voiced

What versions of the chart are there?

There are six versions of the *PronPack Sound Chart*

Chart 1 IPA Phonemic Symbols with Guide Words

This version represents the sounds with letters from the International Phonetics Association (**IPA**) alphabet. The use of this alphabet is widespread in published English Language Teaching material, particularly from British publishers. This is especially useful for dictionary reference. Although many dictionaries are now digital or online and you can click to hear the pronunciation, the ears are often unreliable. Seeing the phonemic spelling will always be very helpful. The guidewords are chosen to show the sounds in context and to show typical English spellings for that sound.

Chart 2 American Symbols with Guide Words

This is a version of the chart using the symbols used in some American textbooks such as *Teaching Pronunciation* (Celce-Murcia, Brinton, Goodwin, CUP 1996).

Chart 3 Typical Spellings with Guide Words

This version is for classes where you feel that the phonemic symbols are not appropriate. Here are some possible scenarios:

- you only have the class for a couple of weeks, and there won't be time to teach the symbols;

- your students are very young and the symbols are too daunting;

- the Roman alphabet is new for your students, and you don't want to make them learn two new alphabets at once.

Using this chart means that even if your students are not familiar with the phonemic symbols, you can still explore the sound system with them.

Chart 4 IPA Phonemic Symbols with Pictures

This version replaces the guide words in **Chart 1** with drawings. When you introduce the chart, identifying what the word is becomes a little task for students to do. Later on, as they get more used to the chart, the drawings become memory pegs – students will associate the sounds with the images, making them more memorable.

Chart 5 American Symbols with Pictures

This is a version of the chart for American English, like **Chart 2** but with pictures instead of guide words.

Chart 6 Typical Spellings with Pictures

This is a version of the chart with typical spellings, like **Chart 3** but with pictures instead of guide words.

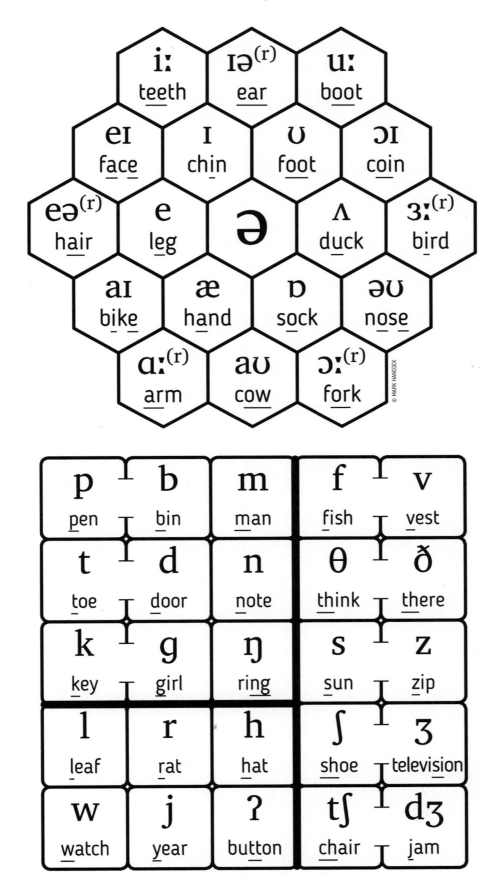

© MARK HANCOCK

Chart 2 American Symbols with Guide Words

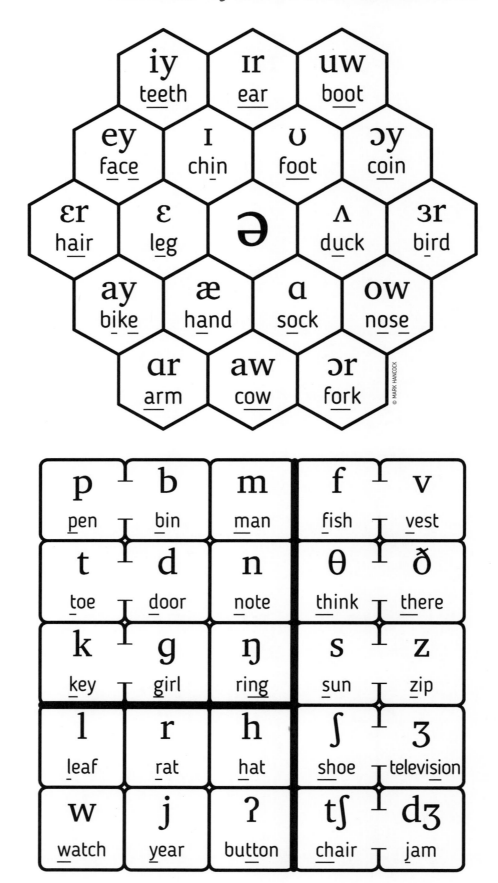

iy teeth	ɪr ear	uw boot	
ey face	ɪ chin	ʊ foot	ɔy coin
ɛr hair	ɛ leg	ə	ʌ duck	ɜr bird
ay bike	æ hand	ɑ sock	ow nose
ɑr arm	aw cow	ɔr fork	

© MARK HANCOCK

p pen	b bin	m man	f fish	v vest
t toe	d door	n note	θ think	ð there
k key	g girl	ŋ ring	s sun	z zip
l leaf	r rat	h hat	ʃ shoe	ʒ television
w watch	j year	ʔ button	tʃ chair	dʒ jam

Chart 3 Typical Spellings with Guide Words

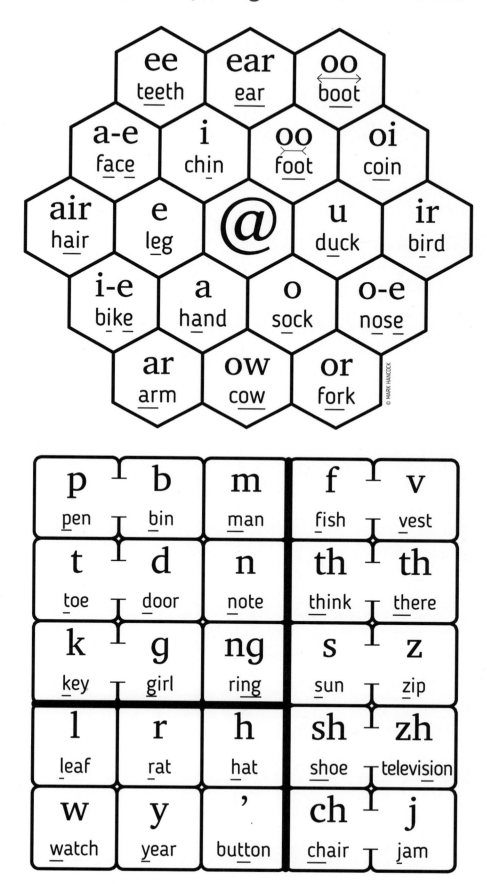

Chart 4 IPA Phonemic Symbols with Pictures

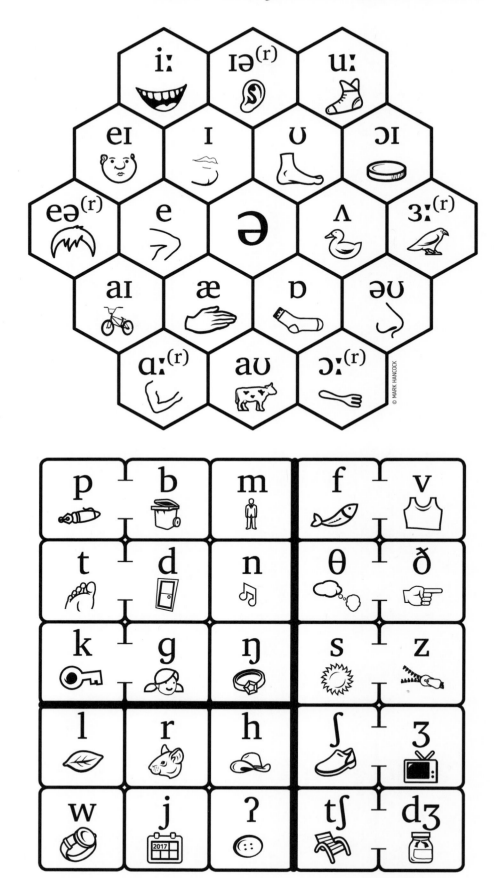

© MARK HANCOCK

Chart 5 American Symbols with Pictures

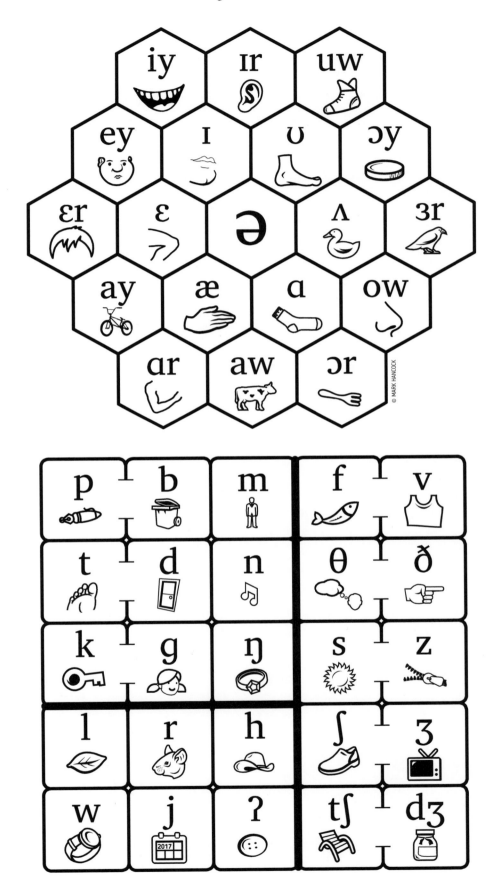

© MARK HANCOCK

Chart 6 Typical Spellings with Pictures

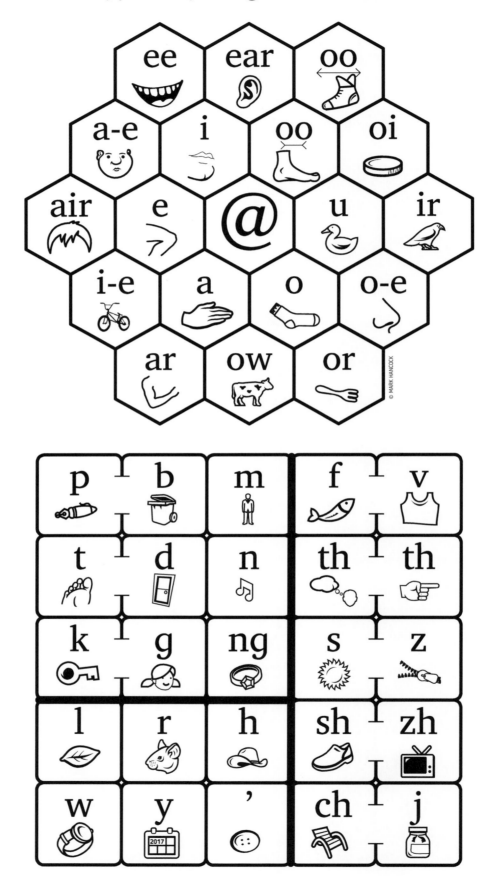

© MARK HANCOCK

PronPack Sound Chart Guided Tour

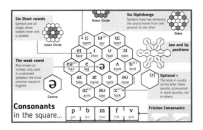

TEACHING FOCUS

To raise awareness of the vowel sound system of English

MINIMUM LEVEL

Elementary upwards

ACTIVITY

Exploring the vowel system of English

WORKSHEETS

PronPack Infographic
PronPack Sound Chart 1
PronPack Sound Chart 2
PronPack Sound Chart 3
PronPack Sound Chart 4
PronPack Sound Chart 5
PronPack Sound Chart 6

AUDIO FILES

No audio with this activity

Background

This activity focuses on the sound system of English and aims to familiarize learners with the system as a whole. Exploring different regions of the PronPack Sound Chart helps the learner become more aware of the articulators in the mouth and vocal tract. For details about how the vowel chart (upper hexagon) and consonant chart (lower square) are organized, see the *Infographic: The PronPack Sound Chart*, page 13.

You could present the vowel and consonant charts separately, on different days, since it is rather a lot to take in at once.

Presentation of the vowel chart

Long vowels

1. Point at /iː/ and make the sound, drawing it out so it is very long. Get your students to copy. Point out that this is the sound to make when you are taking a selfie, because it makes you smile.

   Note: The presentation is based on **PronPack Sound Chart 1**, the *IPA Phonemic Symbols with Guide Words* version. If you are using another version, change accordingly. For example; using **Chart 2**, the *American Symbols* version, it would be – *Point at /iy/*, or using **Chart 3** the *Typical Spellings* version, **Step 1** would be – *Point at /ee/*.

2. Point at /uː/ and make the sound. Get your students to copy. Point out that this is a sound you might make when you get a nice surprise.

3. Point at /ɜː/ and drill the sound. Point out that for this sound, the mouth is completely relaxed. It's the sound we make when we're hesitating, trying to think of what to say next.

4. Point at /ɔː/ and drill the sound. Point out that to make this sound, your mouth must be in the position of a yawn.

5. Point at /ɑː/ and drill the sound. Point out that this is the sound we make at the dentist, because the mouth must be very wide open to make it.

6. Point at /eə/ and drill the sound.

Short vowels and diphthongs

7. Go round the inner circle /ɪ/, /ʊ/, /ɒ/, /ʌ/, /æ/ and /e/, in the same way, but this time exaggerate the shortness of the sounds. Instead of drawing the sound out, cut it short and repeat it several times. Note that when you keep repeating the sound /ʊ/, it sounds like the call of a monkey.

8. Drill the sounds of the diphthongs /ɪə/, /ɔɪ/, /əʊ/, /aʊ/, /aɪ/ and /eɪ/. Point out that for these vowel sounds, the mouth position changes. For example, /eɪ/ begins with the mouth in position for /e/ and moves into the position for /ɪ/.

Unstressed vowel

9. Explain that the central position in the vowel chart is occupied by the sound /ə/. This sound is exceptional because, unlike the others, it is not defined by its quality but by the fact that it only occurs in an unstressed syllable – it is a reduced vowel. For example, it is the first vowel sound in **about**, and the second and third vowel sounds in **Canada**. This is the sound which requires the least effort of all the vowels – the mouth and lip muscles are totally relaxed

Flexi: Although phonemic symbols used are based on a British model, they are not intended to be prescriptive. For instance, /e/ does not specify the precise quality of the vowel, but merely that it is different from neighbouring sounds such as /æ/ or /ɪ/.

alveolar ridge

b

a

tip of tongue

DIAGRAM 1.1-A

Presentation of the consonant chart

1. To raise awareness of the parts of the mouth, copy **DIAGRAM 1.1-A** on the board, without the labelling. Tell students to silently place the tip of their tongues against the edge of the upper teeth. Point to position **a** on the diagram. Now move your finger very slowly from position **a** to position **b** and back on the diagram.

   Ask students to follow this movement with their tongues as they watch. Make sure they are aware of the lump above the teeth (the alveolar ridge) and agree on a name for it – for example, tooth ridge.

Stop consonants

2. Point at the group of sounds /p/, /b/ and /m/ on the consonant chart. Ask students to work out what they have in common (they all involve closing the lips). Point out that if you jump into the pool and you don't want to get water in your mouth, this is a good position for your lips!

3. Point at the group of sounds /t/, /d/ and /n/. Ask students to work out what they have in common (they all involve closing tongue against the alveolar ridge). Point out that if you jump into the pool and you don't want to get water in your mouth, but can't close your lips, this is also a good position!

4. Point at the group of sounds /k/, /g/ and /ŋ/. Ask students to work out what they have in common (they all involve closing the back of the tongue against back of the roof of the mouth). Point out that if you jump into the pool with your mouth open and you don't want to get water in your lungs, this is another a good position!

5. Ask students to say each of the pairs: /p/, /b/; /t/, /d/ and /k/, /g/, with their hand on their throats. They should feel vibration during the second sound of each pair, but not the first.

Friction consonants

6. Point at the two columns on the right side of the consonant chart. Ask students to make these sounds and work out how they are created – what the lips and tongue must do to create the sounds. Note that, with the exception of /tʃ/ and /dʒ/, these sounds can all be elongated indefinitely. In this respect, they differ from /p/, /b/, /t/, /d/ and /k/, /g/, which can only ever be short. The reason /tʃ/ and /dʒ/ cannot be elongated is that /tʃ/ and /dʒ/ are a combination of a stop followed by a friction consonant, as the symbols show. The stop sounds /t/ and /d/ cannot be elongated. Note that there is usually some lip rounding with the sounds /ʃ/, /ʒ/, /tʃ/ and /dʒ/.

7. Ask students to say each of the pairs with their hand on their throats. They should feel vibration during the second sound of each pair, but not the first.

Vowel-like and glottal consonants

8. Point at /l/ and /r/ and ask students to say these sounds and work out what the tongue is doing (the tongue tip touches the alveolar ridge for /l/, but doesn't touch it for /r/)

9. Point at /w/ /j/ and /h/, and ask students to say them and work out how they are created. Note that the /h/ is a friction consonant, produced by narrowing the glottis. Explain that you will not deal with ʔ in today's lesson. This sound is a common alternative pronunciation of /t/, but it is not a separate phoneme in English.

Note: Strictly speaking, the symbols which appear between slanted brackets, such as /ʌ/ or /ʃ/, are phonemes rather than sounds. A phoneme such as /ʌ/ corresponds to slightly different sounds across different accents.

1.1 Goes well with ...

... **PronPack 1.2** and **1.3** for a lesson on the vowel system.

Vowel Chart Pathfinder

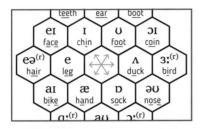

Background

This activity is based on the vowel sounds part of the *PronPack Sound Chart*. Remember that the short vowel sounds occupy the inner circle, while the long vowels and diphthongs occupy the outer circle. The schwa sound is not included in this activity as it doesn't exist in single syllable words out of context.

Presentation

1. Tell students to look at **Chart A** on *Worksheet 1.2*. Say the example words below the symbols from the chart or play *Audio 1.2–1*. Ask students to repeat each word and follow the route with their fingers.

   teeth – ear – boot – face – chin – foot – coin – hair – leg – duck – bird – bike – hand – sock – nose – arm – cow – fork

   (Notice that this route will take their finger in horizontal lines down the chart from top left to bottom right, jumping over the empty middle hexagon).

2. Repeat **Step 1**, but this time creating a different route around the chart or use *Audio 1.2–2* For example:
   hair – bike – hand – foot – ear – teeth – chin – sock – fork – nose – bird – duck – leg – hair

3. Explain to students that, when you say a word from **Chart B**, they should find the vowel sound in it in **Chart A** and say the corresponding word in the hexagon. For example: you say *chair*, students say *hair*; you say *phone*, students say *nose*. Continue with words chosen randomly from hexagons in **Chart B** until students are comfortable with the activity.

Activity

1. Tell students they will follow a route around **Chart A** with a pencil and that the route will start and end at the same hexagon. Explain that the arrows in the central hexagon show how a route may jump across it.

   Ask students to look at **Chart A** and say words from connected hexagons in **Chart B** to create the route or use *Audio 1.2–3*.

For example:

key – pay – check – young – phone – door – brown – match – could – beer - keep

2. Check the answers by asking the class to say the example words on the route they have drawn with their pencils. For the example above, here are the *answers*:

teeth – face – leg – duck – nose – fork – cow – hand – foot – ear - teeth

3. If you think students need more practice to get the hang of this activity, repeat **Steps 4** and **5** with a different route.

4. Put students into **A/B** pairs. Tell Student **A** to look at **Chart A**, and Student **B** to look at **Chart B**. Student **B** is the '*pathfinder*' – he or she must say random words from the hexagons to create a route around the chart. Tell the pathfinder to keep a record of their path with a pencil.

   Student **A** listens and follows the route with a pencil. When they've finished, pairs check answers together.

5. Students swap roles and repeat **Step 4** as many times as you think they need to.

Flexi: You may use the *typical spellings version* (page 17), or the *American Symbols version* (page 16) of the vowel chart for **Student A** if you prefer. This activity should work for most accents – the sound symbols do not represent an exact phonetic quality of the vowels but rather, their place in the system as a whole.

1.2 Goes well with ...

... PronPack **1.1** and **1.3** for a lesson on the vowel system.

Chart A

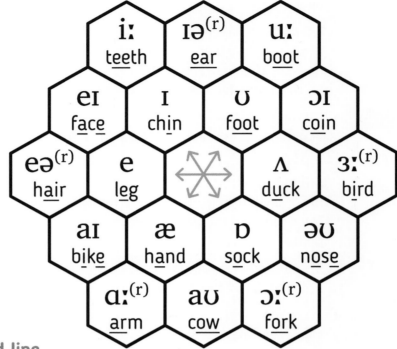

Fold along dotted line

- -

Chart B

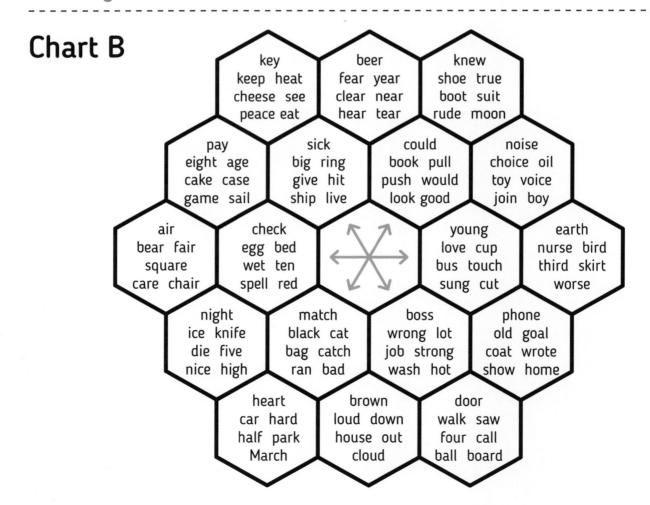

Tongue Cats

1.3

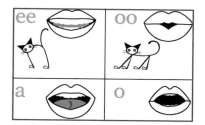

TEACHING FOCUS

To raise awareness of the role of tongue, jaw and lips in vowel sounds

MINIMUM LEVEL

Pre-intermediate

ACTIVITY

Articulation workout; lip reading

WORKSHEETS

PronPack Worksheet 1.3
Print one copy for each student

AUDIO FILES

Background

Vowel sounds are produced by changing the shape of the space inside the mouth. This is done in three ways:

1. moving the body of the tongue up and down, and from front to back;

2. moving the position of the bottom jaw from nearly closed to wide open;

3. moving the lips, from a wide smile to a small round shape.

A cross section of the mouth space is often represented by a square - see **DIAGRAM 1.3A** on the following page. Along the dimension from left to right is the tongue position, from front to back. Along the dimension from top to bottom is jaw position, from closed to open. So, for example, the /ee/ sound in the top left is made with the body of the tongue pushed to the front of the mouth and the jaw nearly closed.

In this activity, we focus on the four vowel sounds closest to the corners in the diagram – in other words, the vowels with the most extreme tongue and jaw positions. We do this in order to make the tongue and jaw movements most noticeable to students and so raise awareness of their importance in creating vowel sounds.

Flexi: If your students are familiar with phonemic symbols, you can write /iː/, /uː/, /æ/ and /ɒ/ into the four corners of the Tongue Cats diagram on the worksheet (or the American symbols /iy/, /uw/, /æ/ and /ɑ/).

Presentation

1. Write the spellings /ee/ and /oo/ on the board, and point out that the slashes show that these refer to sounds. Point to each one and mouth the vowel silently. Get students to say the sounds as you point at the spellings. Move your finger back and forth between them so that the students are saying **eeeeooooeeeeooooooeeeeooooo**.

2. Repeat the activity above, but this time ask students to pay attention to how their tongue is moving. Elicit that the tongue moves back for the /oo/. To demonstrate this, ask students to touch the end of their tongue with a finger or a pencil while they say the two sounds, and notice how it goes further in when they say /oo/.

3. Write the spelling /a/ below the /ee/ on the board. Point at these two in turn and get students to say the sounds. Now ask them to do this again, but this time with the finger of one hand on their nose and the thumb on the chin – see **DIAGRAM 1.3B**. Ask students what they notice, and elicit that the finger and thumb move apart when they move from /ee/ to /a/. Point out that the same thing happens when they move from /oo/ to /o/.

Activity

1. Give out *Worksheet 1.3* and ask students to look at the *Tongue Cats diagram* in the upper half of the page. Explain that the cat represents the tongue. In the top left, it is pushing its body up and forward. In the bottom left, it is pushing down and forward. In the top right, it is pushing up and back. In the bottom right, it is pushing down and back. Get the students to say the sounds in the four boxes, and try to feel how their tongue is moving like the cat in the pictures.

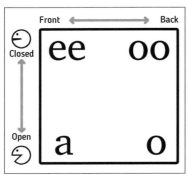

DIAGRAM 1.3A

2. Point out that the jaw is more closed for the sounds in the top two boxes, and more open for the sounds in the bottom two boxes. Remind them of the *finger and thumb test* from the presentation.

3. Point out the lip drawings in each box. Get students to say the sounds and watch their own mouths in a mirror – or in the camera of their phones – to make sure they look like the drawings. Point out that the tongue is visible for the sounds **ee**, **a** and **o**, but not **oo**.

4. Ask students to look at the **word quads** in the bottom half of the worksheet. Point out that they contain the same four vowel sounds, in the same position as in the diagram. Say each group of words rhythmically, getting students to repeat after you, or use *Audio 1.3–1*. Ask them to pay attention to how their mouths are moving as they do this.

   You: *beat... bat... boot... pot*

   Students: *beat... bat... boot... pot*

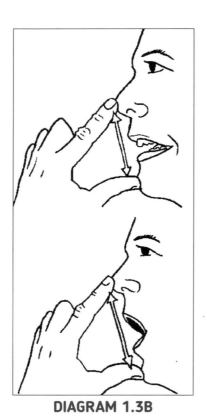

DIAGRAM 1.3B

5. Now ask students to look at **word quad 1**. Explain that you are going to mouth one of the words silently and they have to watch your mouth and lip-read which word you said. Demonstrate this several times.

6. Put students in pairs or small groups. They take it in turns to point to one of the word quads and mouth one of the words silently for the others to lip-read.

1.3 Goes well with ...

... PronPack **1.1** and **1.2** for a lesson on the vowel system.

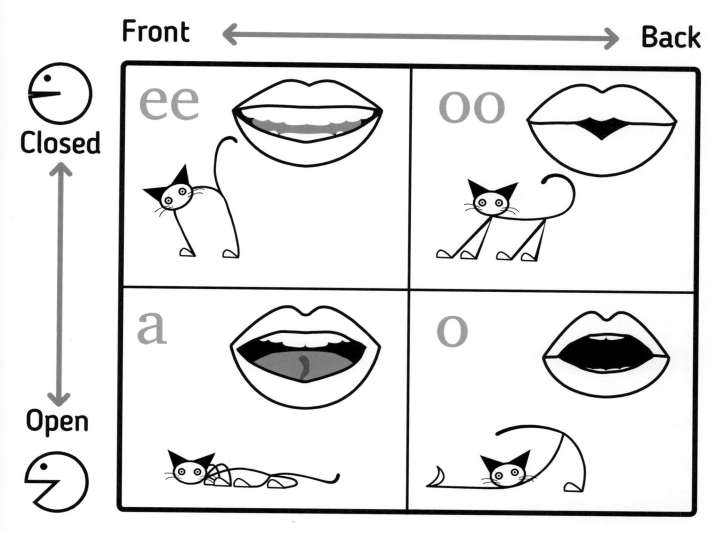

1 beat	boot	**2** read	rude	**3** mean	moon	**4** keep	room
bat	pot	hat	hot	map	pop	gap	rob
5 cheap	tube	**6** least	loose	**7** keys	cool	**8** seat	shoot
jam	job	land	lost	lack	lock	sat	shot
9 feet	food	**10** team	soup	**11** bees	boots	**12** cream	group
fat	fond	tap	top	match	boss	gram	crop

R-Vowel Workout

1.4

	ɪə⁽ʳ⁾ 👂	ɜː⁽ʳ⁾ 🐦	ɔː⁽ʳ⁾	ɑː⁽ʳ⁾	eə⁽ʳ⁾ ⛰
1	ear	earn	or	arm	air
2	beer	bird	board	bar	bear
3	beard	burn	born	barber	bare
4	dear	dirty	door	darling	dare
5	fear	first	four	far	fair
6	feared	firm	form	farm	fare

Background

Of the long vowel sounds and diphthongs in the outer circle of the vowel chart (see **1.1 PronPack Sound Chart Guided Tour**), five have a close relationship to the letter *r*. For example, compare the vowel sound in the words *cat* /æ/ and *cart* /ɑː/. The vowel in *cat* is short, but in *cart* it is long, and the only difference in spelling is the letter *r*, so we can consider the *r* to be a part of the spelling of the vowel sound.

Flexi: Note that the word *cart* can be pronounced /kɑːt/ or /kɑːrt/ depending on accent. For this reason, the /r/ is placed in brackets next to these vowel sounds in the **PronPack Sound Chart**.

Presentation

1. Copy the table below on the board. Say the example words and ask students to pay attention to the difference in the vowel sound in each pair. Point out that the only difference in spelling is the letter *r*.

ɪə	ɜː	ɔː	ɑː	eə
bee - beer	**head - heard**	**spot - sport**	**cat - cart**	**pea - pear**

2. Explain that the effect of the *r* in the spelling of these words is to make the vowel sound longer. There are 5 long vowel sounds which can be created by a following *r*, and these are shown in the table.

Activity

1. Give out *Worksheet 1.4*. Say words **1-15** in each column, asking students to repeat each word after you, or play *Audio 1.4-1*. Note that the same vowel sound should be pronounced in all the words for each column, no matter what the spelling. The picture at the bottom of the row shows the lip position for each sound. Allow students to pronounce the sound /r/ or not, according to which is easier or which accent they prefer. Note that the word *tear* in column 1, row 8, means liquid that comes from your eye when you cry.

2. Now say all five words in each row. Leave a pause at the end of the row for students to repeat the five words. Note that the vowel sound is different in each word.

3. Say the number of a row, and **one** of the words in it. Ask students to identify which word you said by naming the column – first, second, third, fourth or fifth. For example:

You: *1 – arm.*
Students: *Fourth!*

4. Tell students to do **activity 3** in pairs or small groups, with one saying the word and the others naming the column.

5. Tell students to read the example words in each column and make a note of all the possible spellings for each vowel sound. Demonstrate by eliciting or giving the spelling variations for the first column before students continue in pairs or groups.

Here are the *answers* – the most common spelling is given first:

ɪə(r)	ɜː(r)	ɔː(r)	ɑː(r)	eə(r)
eer/ear	er	or/ore	ar	ar/are
ere	ur	our	ear	air
ier	ir	oar/oor	er	ear
	w+or	w+ar		
	ear			
	our			

Note: The sounds /ɜː/ and /eə/ are always spelt with an **r**. There are spellings without **r** for the other sounds. Here are some examples: /ɪə/ - idea; /ɔː/ - caught, call; /ɑː/ - father, calm.

Note: Vowel sounds are shorter when they are followed by a consonant sound, especially if it is unvoiced. For example, **start** and **star** both have the vowel sound /ɑː/, but it is a little shorter in **start**.

Flexi: In General British, the **r** is not pronounced in the words in this activity. In many other accents, including American English, it is. Students can pronounce them as they prefer.

1.4 Goes well with ...

... **PronPack 2.2** and **PronPack 4.3** for a lesson on r-coloured vowels.

	Iə(r) 👂	3ː(r) 🐦	ɔː(r) 🍴	ɑː(r) 💪	eə(r) 🔥
1	ear	earn	or	arm	air
2	beer	bird	board	bar	bear
3	beard	burn	born	barber	bare
4	dear	dirty	door	darling	dare
5	fear	first	four	far	fair
6	feared	firm	form	farm	fare
7	pier	purse	port	part	pear
8	tear (n)	turn	tour	tart	tear (v)
9	steer	serve	store	star	stair
10	hear	heard	horse	heart	hair
11	cheers	shirt	short	chart	chairs
12	gears	girl	course	card	cares
13	near	nurse	north	March	Mary
14	year	journey	your	jar	share
15	here	word	warm	hard	wear

Alphabet Vowel Workout

1.5

eɪ	iː	aɪ	əʊ	(j)u
eight	eat	ice	old	use
bay	beat	bite	boat	boot
pays	peas	pies	pose	pool
main	mean	mine	moan	moon
take	tea	tie	toe	tune

TEACHING FOCUS

To raise awareness of vowel distinctions and sound-spelling patterns

MINIMUM LEVEL

Pre-intermediate

ACTIVITY

Articulation workout; spelling pattern spotting

WORKSHEETS

PronPack Worksheet 1.5
Print one copy for each student

AUDIO FILES

Background

There are five vowel letters in the English alphabet, and the names of these letters are all long vowels or diphthongs from the outer circle of the vowel chart (see **1.1 PronPack Sound Chart Guided Tour**):

eɪ	iː	aɪ	əʊ	(j)uː
A	E	I	O	U

In spelling, these sounds are often represented by two vowel letters (**ma_in**), a vowel letter plus **y** or **w** (**ma_y**, **mo_w**), or a vowel letter plus a **silent e** after the following consonant (**ma_ne**). Spellings with two vowel letters can be problematic for students because they often have many different possible pronunciations – particularly the spellings **ea** and **ou**.

Notice that the alphabet name for the letter **u** has the consonant sound /j/ in it. This is sometimes pronounced in words containing **u** (**cute**), and sometimes not (**rude**).

Presentation

Write the five vowel letters on the board and elicit from students how they are pronounced in the alphabet. Write the phonemic transcriptions next to each letter. Point out that there is the consonant sound /j/ in the alphabet name of **u**.

Activity

1. Give out *Worksheet 1.5*. Say words **1-15** in each column, asking students to repeat each word after you, or play *Audio 1.5-1*. Note that the same vowel sound should be pronounced in all the words for each column, no matter what the spelling.

2. Ask students to identify which of the words in the **u** column contain the consonant sound /j/ (*use, tune, knew, cute*).

Flexi: In American English, the /j/ is not pronounced in *tune* and *knew*)

3. Now say all five words in each row. Leave a pause at the end of the row for students to repeat the five words. Note that the vowel sound is different in each word.

4. Tell students to read the example words in each column and make a note of all the possible spellings for each vowel sound. Demonstrate by eliciting or giving the spelling variations for the first column before students continue in pairs or groups.

Here are the *answers*:

eɪ	iː	aɪ	əʊ	(j)uː
a-e	*ee/ea*	*i-e*	*o/o-e*	*u-e*
ai/ay	*e-e*	*ie*	*oe*	*oo*
ei	*e*	*i/y*	*oa*	*ou*
	ie	*ig/igh*	*ow*	*oe*
				ue

Note: Vowel sounds are shorter when they are followed by an unvoiced consonant sound. For example, **beat** and **bee** both have the vowel sound /iː/, but it is a little shorter in **beat**.

1.5 Goes well with ...

... **PronPack 2.2** Version 5, **2.12** and **PronPack 4.4** for a lesson on vowels spelt with two letters.

1.5 Alphabet Vowel Workout

eɪ	iː	aɪ	əʊ	(j)uː
1 eight	eat	ice	old	use
2 bay	beat	bite	boat	boot
3 pays	peas	pies	pose	pool
4 main	mean	mine	moan	moon
5 take	tea	tie	toe	tune
6 tray	tree	try	throw	true
7 name	knee	night	know	knew
8 cake	keep	kite	coat	cute
9 failed	field	filed	fold	fooled
10 sane	scene	sign	soap	soup
11 shave	she	shy	show	shoe
12 chain	cheese	child	chose	choose
13 rate	read	right	wrote	rude
14 hate	heat	high	home	whose
15 wake	week	while	woke	wound
A	**E**	**I**	**O**	**U**

Short Vowel Workout

1.6

æ 🤚	e ☝️	ɪ 👃	ɒ 🧦	ʌ 🦆	ʊ 🦶
pack	pet	pick	pot	pub	put
bat	best	bit	box	bus	book
badly	bury	busy	bottle	butter	butcher
mad	mess	miss	not	nut	bull
tan	ten	tip	top	touch	took
dad	dead	did	dog	duck	could

TEACHING FOCUS

To raise awareness of short vowel distinctions and sound-spelling patterns

MINIMUM LEVEL

Pre-intermediate

ACTIVITY

Articulation workout; spelling pattern spotting

WORKSHEETS

PronPack Worksheet 1.6
Print one copy for each student

AUDIO FILES

Background

The six short vowels occupy the inner circle of the vowel chart (see **1.1 PronPack Sound Chart Guided Tour**). They are also known as *lax* vowels, because the mouth muscles are more relaxed than in the long vowels of the outer circle – which are also known as *tense vowels.* Short vowels are usually spelt with a single vowel letter, with no *silent e* after the following consonant – compare *cut* (short) with *cute* (long), for example. There must always be a consonant sound after a short vowel, and often this is spelt with two consonant letters – compare *ridden* (the *i* is a short vowel) with *rider* (the *i* is a long vowel), for example. In other words, the doubled consonant letter serves to show that the vowel before it is short.

Presentation

Copy the table below on the board. Say the example words. Point out that each letter of the alphabet has two typical pronunciations – as in the alphabet – and a short equivalent.

The table shows this clearly. It also shows that the letter *U* has two typical short sounds, so there are a total of six short vowel sounds.

	A	**E**	**I**	**O**	**U**	
Alphabet vowel	eɪ *hate*	iː *Pete*	aɪ *hide*	əʊ *note*	(j)uː *cute*	
Short vowel	æ *hat*	e *pet*	ɪ *hid*	ɒ *not*	ʌ *cut*	ʊ *put*

Activity

1. Give out *Worksheet 1.6*. Say words **1-15** in each of the six columns, asking students to repeat each word after you, or play *Audio 1.6-1*.

   Note that the same vowel sound should be pronounced in all the words for each column, no matter what the spelling. The picture at the bottom of the row shows the lip position for each sound. Make sure that students say all these sounds short – exaggerate the shortness when you model the words.

2. Now say all **six** words in each row. Leave a pause at the end of the row for students to repeat the six words. Note that the vowel sound is different in each word.

3. Say the number of a row (**1-15**), and <u>**one**</u> of the words in it. Ask students to identify which word you said by naming the column – *first, second, third, fourth, fifth* or *sixth*. For example:

You: *1 – put.*
Students: *Sixth!*

4. Tell students to repeat the activity in **Step 3** working in pairs or small groups, with one saying the word and the others naming the column.

5. Tell students to read the example words in each column and make a note of all the possible spellings for each vowel sound. Demonstrate by eliciting or giving the spelling variations for the first column before students continue in pairs or groups.

Here are the *answers* – the most common spelling is given first:

æ	e	ɪ	ɒ	ʌ	ʊ
a	e	i	o	u	u
	ea	u	w+a	o	oo
	u		a+l	ou	oul

Note: Short vowel sounds are shorter when they are followed by an unvoiced consonant sound. For example, **man** and **map** both have the vowel sound /æ/, but it is a little shorter in **map**.

Flexi: The short vowel /ɒ/ does not exist in an American accent: /ɑ/is used – like /ɑː/ but not as long. You may wish to modify the worksheet for American symbols. Cross out the /e/ and /ɒ/ symbols and replace them with /ɛ/ and /ɑ/.

1.6 Goes well with ...

... **PronPack 2.3, PronPack 3.1** Version 2, **3.3** vowel pairs and **PronPack 4.2** for a lesson on short vowels.

	æ	e	ɪ	ɒ	ʌ	ʊ
1	pack	pet	pick	pot	pub	put
2	bat	best	bit	box	bus	book
3	badly	bury	busy	bottle	butter	butcher
4	mad	mess	miss	not	nut	bull
5	tan	ten	tip	top	touch	took
6	dad	dead	did	dog	duck	could
7	cat	kept	kiss	cost	cup	cook
8	gas	guess	gift	gone	gun	good
9	fat	felt	fit	fog	fun	full
10	sand	send	sink	sock	son	sugar
11	stand	spell	slim	salt	stuff	should
12	land	lemon	lift	lock	luck	look
13	rat	red	ring	wrong	rung	would
14	hand	head	hill	hot	honey	hood
15	wax	west	wind	want	won	wood

Stop Consonant Workout

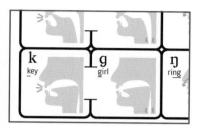

TEACHING FOCUS

To raise awareness of the plosives and nasals

MINIMUM LEVEL

Pre-intermediate

ACTIVITY

Exploring the plosives and nasal consonants; a minimal pair activity

WORKSHEETS

PronPack Worksheet 1.7
Print one copy for each student

AUDIO FILES

No audio with this activity

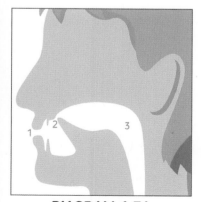

DIAGRAM 1.7A

Background

The block of nine consonant sounds in the top left of the sound chart all require complete closure of the airway through the mouth. The airway can be stopped in one of the three places numbered in the **DIAGRAM 1.7A**. They are 'watertight' because, if you jumped into a pool, you could stop the water going down your throat by closing the mouth in any of these places!

In the case of the plosive consonants /p/, /b/, /t/, /d/, /k/ and /g/, there is a moment of complete silence when the airway is closed. In the case of the nasals /m/, /n/ and /ŋ/, the air is stopped through the mouth but escapes through the nose instead. If you hold your nose, the sound will stop.

The main problems for students are distinguishing the voiced and unvoiced pairs of plosives, and distinguishing the three nasal sounds – particularly at the end of a word.

Presentation

1. Demonstrate the sounds /p/ and /b/. Suspend a sheet of paper in front of your mouth and show how it is blown by the air from your mouth when you say /p/ but not when you say /b/. Put your hand on your throat and explain that you can feel vibration when you say /b/ but not when you say /p/. This puff of air is known as aspiration. Get students to try these experiments for themselves.

2. Give out *Worksheet 1.7*. Ask students to look at the top half of the page and match statements **1-6** with the name of a **column** or **row** of the chart, using the pictures to help them.

   Here are the *answers*:

   Statement **1** = *row* **c**
   Statement **2** = *column* **3**
   Statement **3** = *row* **a**
   Statement **4** = *column* **1**
   Statement **5** = *row* **b**
   Statement **6** = *column* **1**

Activity

1. Ask students to look at **Grid 1** in the bottom half of the page. Say **words** from the grid at random and ask students to say the number of the word you are saying. For example:

   You: *bride*
   Students: *Five!*
   You: *pet*
   Students: *Three!*

2. Put students in pairs or groups of three. Students take turns to do as you demonstrated in **Step 1** above: One student says a **word 1-6** from **Grid 1** at random and the others say which number they heard. They should try to get five correctly understood consecutively before swapping roles for the other student(s) to take a turn at speaking.

3. When all students in a pair or group have had a turn saying the words in **Grid 1**, ask them to put a tick in the box and move on to **Grid 2**. When they have finished **Grid 2**, they put a tick in the box and move on to **Grid 3** and so on.

4. Ask the class to say which grid they found the most difficult.

1.7 Goes well with ...

... **PronPack 3.3** consonant pairs, **3.4** Version 1, and **PronPack 4.11** for a lesson on stop consonants.

1 The back of the tongue closes the gap. = row **c**

2 The air comes out of the nose.

3 The top and the bottom lips close the gap.

4 There is no vibration in the throat.

5 The tongue tip touches the back of the top gum.

6 There's a small puff of air from the mouth.

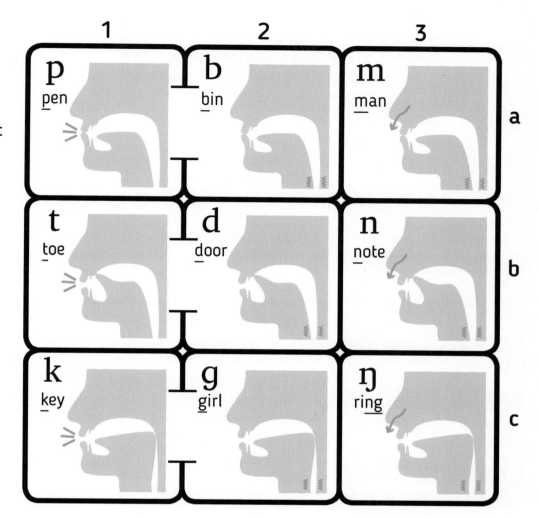

	1	2	3
a	p pen	b bin	m man
b	t toe	d door	n note
c	k key	g girl	ŋ ring

1

1 bed	2 bet	3 pet
4 bright	5 bride	6 pride

☐

2

1 gun	2 gum	3 come
4 gain	5 game	6 came

☐

3

1 goat	2 coat	3 code
4 cab	5 cap	6 gap

☐

4

1 bag	2 back	3 pack
4 big	5 pig	6 pick

☐

5

1 sun	2 sum	3 sung
4 mine	5 mime	6 nine

☐

6

1 tight	2 tied	3 died
4 bad	5 pad	6 pat

☐

Friction Consonant Workout

1.8

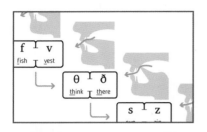

TEACHING FOCUS

To raise awareness of the fricative consonants

MINIMUM LEVEL

Pre-intermediate

ACTIVITY

Exploring the fricatives; a minimal pair activity

WORKSHEETS

PronPack Worksheet 1.8
Print one copy for each student

AUDIO FILES

No audio with this activity

Background

The two columns of sounds on the right hand side of the consonant part of the **PronPack Sound Chart** are known as fricatives (The final pair /tʃ/ and /dʒ/ are a combination of stop and fricative, and are not dealt with in this lesson). The fricatives are organized into pairs of sounds, with the unvoiced sounds in the left hand column and the voiced equivalents in the neighbouring right hand column. These four pairs of sounds are reproduced at the top of the worksheet for this lesson.

In fricative consonants, the sound is caused by the friction of air passing through a narrowing of the airway. The narrowing is created in four possible places: with the top teeth and bottom lip for /f/ and /v/; with the teeth and tongue tip for /θ/ and /ð/; with the tongue and alveolar ridge for /s/ and /z/, and with the tongue and roof of the mouth for /ʃ/ and /ʒ/. These four positions are illustrated on the worksheet. Note that /h/ is also a fricative consonant, but it is not dealt with in this activity.

Presentation

1. Give out *Worksheet 1.8*. Ask students to look at the **illustrations** at the top of the page. Make one long continuous unvoiced sound, moving your mouth gradually from the position on the left to the position on the right, like this: /ffffθθθθssssʃʃʃʃ/. Tell your students to copy, paying attention to how their tongue is moving as they do so.

   Now do the same, but with voicing: /vvvvððððzzzzʒʒʒʒ/. Tell your students to do this with their hand on their throat so that they can feel the vibration.

2. Notice that if your students have a problem with the sound /ʃ/, they may find it easier to produce with some lip rounding, in addition to the tongue position shown in the illustration. Notice that the sound /ʒ/ is not common in English, and there are no examples in the activity.

Activity

1. Ask students to look at **Grid 1** in the bottom half of the page. Say **words** from the grid at random and ask students to say the number of the word you are saying. For example:

   You: *lived*
   Students: *Five!*
   You: *than*
   Students: *Three!*

2. Put students in pairs or groups of three. Students take turns to do as you demonstrated in **Step 1** above: One student says a **word 1-6** at random and the others say which number they heard. They should try to get five correctly understood consecutively, before swapping roles for the other student(s) to take a turn at speaking.

3. When all students in a pair or group have had a turn saying the words in **Grid 1**, ask them to put a tick in the box and move on to **Grid 2**. When they have finished **Grid 2**, they put a tick in the box and move on to **Grid 3** and so on.

4. Ask the class to say which grid they found the most difficult.

Flexi: Many speakers of English do not pronounce the sounds /θ/ and /ð/, replacing them with /t/ and /d/ or /f/ and /v/. Consequently, if your students do the same, it probably will not make them unintelligible.

1.8 Goes well with ...

... PronPack 2.2 Version 2, **PronPack 3.3** consonant pairs, **3.4** Version 3, **PronPack 4.9** and **4.10** for a lesson on fricatives and affricates.

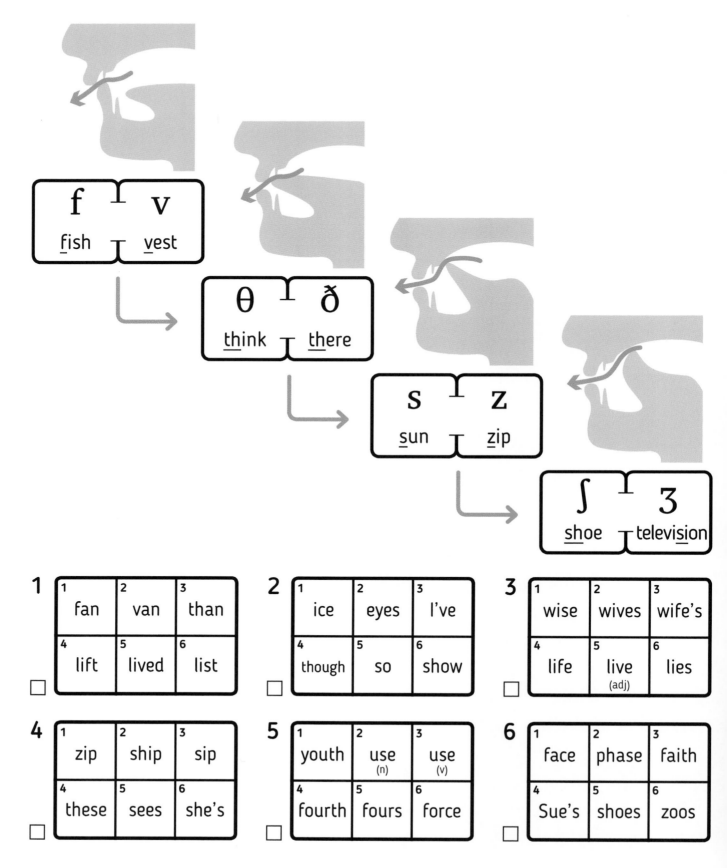

f	**v**
<u>f</u>ish	<u>v</u>est

θ	**ð**
<u>th</u>ink	<u>th</u>ere

s	**z**
<u>s</u>un	<u>z</u>ip

ʃ	**ʒ**
<u>sh</u>oe	televi<u>s</u>ion

1

1 fan	2 van	3 than
4 lift	5 lived	6 list

2

1 ice	2 eyes	3 I've
4 though	5 so	6 show

3

1 wise	2 wives	3 wife's
4 life	5 live (adj)	6 lies

4

1 zip	2 ship	3 sip
4 these	5 sees	6 she's

5

1 youth	2 use (n)	3 use (v)
4 fourth	5 fours	6 force

6

1 face	2 phase	3 faith
4 Sue's	5 shoes	6 zoos

Cluster Clocks

1.9

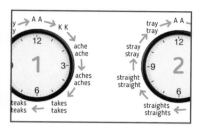

TEACHING FOCUS

To raise awareness of syllable structure and practise consonant clusters

MINIMUM LEVEL

Pre-intermediate

ACTIVITY

A choral chant/drill

WORKSHEETS

PronPack Worksheet 1.9
Print one copy for each student

AUDIO FILES

Background

An English syllable consists of a vowel sound, either on its own as in the word **eye** /aɪ/ or with consonant sounds before as in **tie** /taɪ/, after as in **eyes** /aɪz/ or both as in **ties** /taɪz/. There may be up to three consonant sounds before the vowel sound, as in **street** /striːt/, and up to four at the end, as in **sixths** /sɪksθs/. Combinations of consonants like this are known as consonant clusters, and these may present pronunciation difficulties for some students.

The **Cluster Clocks** in this activity are circles of 1-syllable words. At 12 o'clock, we see the simplest possible syllable consisting of a vowel sound only. As we move round to 6 o'clock, the syllable gets increasingly complex, with consonants added to the beginning and end of the syllable. As we move back round to 12 o'clock, these consonants are gradually removed again. In this activity, students listen and repeat the words around the circle, keeping to a **tick tock** rhythm. Each word is repeated twice in the circle.

Presentation

Write the **words** and /**symbols**/ below on the board. The symbols should not be a problem even if your students are not used to them because, in this example, their meaning is quite transparent.

Explain that all the words have one vowel sound. Ask the students to count the consonant sounds in each name or word. Elicit the number. Represent each consonant sound with a **C**, and each vowel sound with a *V* (as below).

A /eɪ/ *V*	**K** /keɪ/ *CV*	**ache** /eɪk/ *VC*
aches /eɪks/ *VCC*	**takes** /teɪks/ *CVCC*	**steaks** /steɪks/ *CCVCC*
steak /steɪk/ *CCVC*	**stay** /steɪ/ *CCV*	**say** /seɪ/ *CV*

Activity

1. Give out *Worksheet 1.9* and ask students to look at **Clock 1**. Ask half the class to create a rhythm by saying **tick tock (pause, pause) tick tock (pause, pause)**. Tell the rest of the students to repeat the words around the clock after you in the pauses.

Alternatively, use *Audio 1.9-1*:

You: *A A*
Students: *A A*
You: *K K*
Students: *K K*
You: *ache*
Students: *ache*

2. Get students to switch roles, so the group which was saying **tick tock** now repeats after you and the others say **tick tock (pause, pause)**. Go around the clock again.

3. Repeat the activity with the rest of the clocks, or vary the procedure by asking volunteers to lead and the others to repeat, as a class or in groups.

Flexi: Speakers often simplify consonant clusters at the end of a word. For example, in "*smiles smiles*", the **s** at the end of the first word simply joins together with the **s** at the beginning of the next, so that it sounds like "*smile smiles*".

1.9 Goes well with ...

... **PronPack 4.13** for a lesson on consonant clusters.

Clock 1: say say → A A → K K → ache ache → aches aches → takes takes → steaks steaks → steak steak → stay stay

Clock 2: tray tray → A A → say say → stay stay → state state → states states → straights straights → straight straight → stray stray

Clock 3: rare rare → air air → where where → swear swear → swears swears → squares squares → square square → scare scare → care care

Clock 4: see see → E E → key key → keep keep → peak peak → peaks peaks → speaks speaks → speak speak → seek seek

Clock 5: lie lie → I I → my my → mile mile → smile smile → smiles smiles → miles miles → limes limes → lime lime

Clock 6: eat eat → E E → tea tea → tree tree → treat treat → street street → streets streets → treats treats → eats eats

Word Stress Workout

●●●	**Hair**dressers	**stud**ying	**re**cipes.
●●●	De**sign**ers	ex**chang**ing	um**brel**las.
●●●	Employ**ees**	recom**mend**	maga**zines**.
●●●	**Won**derful	**Af**rican	**el**ephants.
●●●	Un**hap**py	Nor**we**gian	go**ril**las.
●●●	Impo**lite**	Portu**guese**	chimpan**zee**
●●●	**Bus**inessmen	**rec**ognize	**mess**ages.
●●●	De**tec**tives	re**mem**ber	ac**count**ant
●●●	Volun**teers**	under**stand**	millio**naires**

TEACHING FOCUS

To raise awareness of word stress

MINIMUM LEVEL

Intermediate

ACTIVITY

Choral chant/drill

WORKSHEETS

PronPack Worksheet 1.10
Print one copy for each student

AUDIO FILES

Background

Stress is an important part of the sound of a word in English, and it does not always fall on the same syllable, as it does in some other languages. All of the words in this activity consist of three syllables. For a 3-syllable word, there are three possible stress patterns: **Ooo, oOo** or **ooO** (stress on the first syllable, stress on the second syllable or stress on the third syllable).

Word stress is created by making one syllable stronger – longer, louder and higher in pitch, and the other syllables weaker – often, but not always, by reducing the vowel sounds.

Presentation

1. Write the three tourism slogans below on the board and say them aloud. Ask students to stay how many syllables each word has (*3 in each word*) and which syllable is stressed in the adjectives and names of countries (*a = 1st* **Ooo**, *b = 2nd* **oOo** and *c = 3rd* **ooO**).

   a Fabulous Portugal!

   b Fantastic Jamaica!

   c Picturesque Pakistan!

2. Say the phrases and ask the class to repeat. Then continue, mixing up the phrases at random, e.g. *Fabulous Pakistan!*; *Fantastic Portugal!*; *Picturesque Jamaica…*

3. Now say just the letters and ask students to say the phrases, e.g.:

   You: *a a*
   Students: *Fabulous Portugal!*

   You: *a b*
   Students: *Fabulous Jamaica!*

   You: *a c*
   Students: *Fabulous Pakistan!*

Activity

1. Give out *Worksheet 1.10* and ask students to focus only on **Block 1** for now. Point out that the letters in bold are the stressed syllables.

   Explain that you will say the letters and they have to say the sentences, e.g.:

   a a a = **Hair**dressers **stud**ying **re**cipes.

   b b b = De**sign**ers ex**chang**ing um**brell**as.

   c c c = Employ**ees** reco**mmend** maga**zines**.

   Repeat each line several times.

   Optional: Use *Audio 1.10-1* to hear all of the lines in **Blocks 1-5**.

2. Repeat **Step 1**, but this time clapping a rhythm of four beats:

	clap	clap	clap	clap
You:	*a*	*a*	*a*	
	clap	clap	clap	clap
Students:	*Hairdressers*	*studying*	*recipes.*	

   The stressed syllables in each of the students' words should fall on the beat which is marked by the clap. The fourth clap is a silence.

3. Repeat **Step 2**, but now mix up the sentences, e.g.:

	clap	clap	clap	clap
You:	*c*	*a*	*b*	
	clap	clap	clap	clap
Students:	*Employees*	*studying*	*umbrellas.*	

4. Repeat the drill with the other blocks on the sheet, or get volunteers from the class to take the teacher's role and give letter combinations for their classmates to 'translate'.

Flexi: In American English, some of the **ooO** words in this activity are stressed on the first syllable instead (*Pakistan, millionaire, magazine*) or on the second syllable (*employee, chimpanzee*). More generally, speakers sometimes move stress away from the last syllable of a word if the next word begins with a stressed syllable, for example "**sev**enteen <u>six</u>ty" instead of "seven<u>teen</u> <u>six</u>ty". This is known as *stress shift*.

1.10 Goes well with ...

... **PronPack 2.7**, **PronPack 3.8** and **PronPack 4.16** for a lesson on word stress families.

1
a	●●●	**Hair**dressers	**stud**ying	**re**cipes.
b	●●●	De**sign**ers	ex**chang**ing	um**brell**as.
c	●●●	Employ**ees**	reco**mmend**	maga**zines**.

2
a	●●●	**Won**derful	**Af**rican	**el**ephants.
b	●●●	Un**happ**y	Nor**weg**ian	go**rill**as.
c	●●●	Impo**lite**	Portu**guese**	chimpan**zees**.

3
a	●●●	**Bus**inessmen	**re**cognize	**mess**ages.
b	●●●	De**tec**tives	re**mem**ber	a**count**ants.
c	●●●	Volun**teers**	under**stand**	millio**naires**.

4
a	●●●	**Beaut**iful	**Mex**ican	**ap**ricots.
b	●●●	De**lic**ious	Mo**rocc**an	to**mat**oes.
c	●●●	Imma**ture**	Leba**nese**	tange**rines**.

5
a	●●●	**Sev**enty	**inter**esting	**veh**icles.
b	●●●	E**lev**en	ex**pen**sive	com**put**ers.
c	●●●	Seven**teen**	second **hand**	servi**ettes**.

Bricks and Mortar

1.11

ONE to TWO to THREE to FOUR		ONE as a TWO as a THREE as a FOUR
		ONE out of TWO out of THREE out of FOUR
	Level 2	
ONE of his TWO of his THREE of his FOUR		ONE for a TWO for a THREE for a FOUR
NE of their TWO of their THREE of their FOUR		ONE for my TWO for my THREE for my FOUR
ONE of my TWO of my THREE of my FOUR		ONE into TWO into THREE into FOUR
NE of your TWO of your THREE of your FOUR		ONE as if TWO as if THREE as if FOUR
ONE of our TWO of our THREE of our FOUR		ONE there are TWO there are THREE there are FO
ONE of the TWO of the THREE of the FOUR		ONE that was TWO that was THREE that was FO
	Level 3	

TEACHING FOCUS

To raise awareness of weak forms and practise connected speech

MINIMUM LEVEL

Pre-intermediate to Intermediate

ACTIVITY

Choral chant/drill

WORKSHEETS

PronPack Worksheet 1.11
Print one copy for each student

AUDIO FILES

Background

The most common words in English are the function words – see the content/function table below with examples in brackets. The words are usually reduced to weak forms in speech, and they blend together. They are also unstressed.

Content words (Bricks)	Function words (Mortar)
nouns (*hour*, *tea*)	prepositions (*to*, *for*)
main verbs (*play*, *wait*)	the verb *to be* (*is*, *are*, *was*)
adjectives and adverbs (*good*, *quickly*)	auxiliary verbs (*can*, *does*)
	articles (*an*, *the*)
question words (*who*, *what*)	conjunctions (*and*, *or*)
	personal pronouns (*you*, *her*)

In this chant, the content words are replaced by numbers **one** to **four**, and these fall on the beat of the rhythm. These are joined by many different and common combinations of function words which fall between the beats of the rhythm.

Presentation

1. Write the phrases below on the board and say them aloud. Make sure you reduce the word ***to*** so that it contrasts clearly with the word ***two***.

   One two three

   One to three

2. Point out that ***two*** is stressed because it is a ***content word*** and ***to*** is unstressed because it is a ***function word***. Give more examples of function words from the function/content table above.

3. Explain the *bricks and mortar* metaphor: the content words are like the bricks and the function words are like the mortar which joins the bricks together.

Activity

1. Decide how much of the chant on the *Worksheet 1.11* you want to use. If level **1** is too simple, miss out that level. If level **3** is too difficult, miss out that level.

2. Say the chant, and leave a gap after each line for your students to repeat, or use *Audio 1.11–1*.

   Try to maintain the same rhythm, with the numbers falling on the beat and the function words squeezing into the space between.

3. Pay attention to lines that your students seem to find difficult to say. Return to these at the end and drill them more slowly. If necessary, point out features which the students may not have noticed – for example, the **t** is cut in **must**.

More ideas

Ask students to replace the numbers in the workout with 1-syllable words (nouns, verbs or adjectives etc.). The whole sentence does not need to make sense, but part of it should, such as *milk could be cheese*.

For example:

Milk or eggs or cheese or fruit

Milk could be cheese could be cream could be cake

If your students can't think of any ideas, here are some words you could suggest:

milk, eggs, cheese, cream, fruit, rice, wine, meat, fish, cake, bread	hands, feet, knees, toes, socks, shoes, arms, hands, head	blue, green, black, white, brown, red, late, free, fine, sad, small, big, long, short
Sam, Anne, Dave, Jane, Joe, Sue	France, Spain, Wales, Rome, Greece, Prague	clouds, bees, trees, birds
this, that, here, there, up, down, left, right	you, me, mine, hers, ours, theirs	got, went, stopped, sat, watched, saw, met

1.11 Goes well with ...

... **PronPack 2.4** Version 2, **PronPack 4.5** and **4.17** for a lesson on weak forms.

1.11 Bricks and Mortar

Level 1

ONE or TWO or THREE or FOUR
ONE and TWO and THREE and FOUR
ONE at TWO at THREE at FOUR
ONE by TWO by THREE by FOUR
ONE to TWO to THREE to FOUR

ONE or a TWO or a THREE or a FOUR
ONE and a TWO and a THREE and a FOUR
ONE and her TWO and her THREE and her FOUR
ONE and the TWO and the THREE and the FOUR
ONE as a TWO as a THREE as a FOUR
ONE out of TWO out of THREE out of FOUR

Level 2

ONE of his TWO of his THREE of his FOUR
ONE of their TWO of their THREE of their FOUR
ONE of my TWO of my THREE of my FOUR
ONE of your TWO of your THREE of your FOUR
ONE of our TWO of our THREE of our FOUR
ONE of the TWO of the THREE of the FOUR

ONE for a TWO for a THREE for a FOUR
ONE for my TWO for my THREE for my FOUR
ONE into TWO into THREE into FOUR
ONE as if TWO as if THREE as if FOUR
ONE there are TWO there are THREE there are FOUR
ONE that was TWO that was THREE that was FOUR

Level 3

ONE is a TWO is a THREE is a FOUR
ONE was in TWO was in THREE was in FOUR
ONE 'll be TWO 'll be THREE 'll be FOUR
ONE did a TWO did a THREE did a FOUR
ONE does a TWO does a THREE does a FOUR
ONE has been TWO has been THREE has been FOUR

ONE isn't TWO isn't THREE isn't FOUR
ONE wasn't TWO wasn't THREE wasn't FOUR
ONE 'd be TWO 'd be THREE 'd be FOUR
ONE can be TWO can be THREE can be FOUR
ONE could be TWO could be THREE could be FOUR
ONE must be TWO must be THREE must be FOUR

Rhythm Workout

●	Where's	Dave's	lunch?
●●	Where was	Marta's	party?
●●●	Who was at	Jennifer's	barbecue?

TEACHING FOCUS

To raise awareness of rhythm

MINIMUM LEVEL

Pre-intermediate

ACTIVITY

Choral chant/drill

WORKSHEETS

PronPack Worksheet 1.12
Print one copy for each student

AUDIO FILES

Background

English words can be classified into content words and function words:

Content words	Function words
nouns (**hour, tea**)	prepositions (**to, for**)
main verbs (**play, wait**)	the verb **to be** (**is, are, was**)
adjectives and adverbs (**good, quickly**)	auxiliary verbs (**can, does**)
	articles (**an, the**)
question words (**who, what**)	conjunctions (**and, or**)
	personal pronouns (**you, her**)

When words are combined into phrases, the stressed syllables of the content words are pronounced strongly while the remaining syllables and the function words are pronounced weakly, often squeezed into the spaces between the strong syllables. The tendency for weak syllables to be squeezed often gives students the impression that English is hard to understand because it is spoken very quickly. This activity will help students to become aware of the rhythm of the language.

Presentation

1. Write the three example sentences on the board.

   a   *Where's Dave's lunch?* **OOO**

   b   *Where was Marta's party?* **OoOoOo**

   c   *Who was at Jennifer's barbecue?* **OooOooOoo**

   Say them aloud and get students to repeat. Elicit the number of syllables in each sentence and ask students to say which ones are pronounced strongly. Show how the syllables can be represented by circles – big for strong syllables and small for weak syllables. Explain that because of the different stress patterns the three sentences have a different rhythm from each other.

2. Point out that weak syllables may be unstressed syllables which are part of a longer word, for example the second syllable in *party*, or a whole word, for example *was* in the phrase *Where was Marta*?

Activity

1. Give out *Worksheet 1.12* and ask students to focus only on **Block 1** for now. Point out that the letters in bold are the stressed syllables.

   Explain that you will say the letters and they have to say the sentences, e.g.:

   a a a = *Where's Dave's lunch?*;
   b b b = *Where was Marta's party?*;
   c c c = *Who was at Jennifer's barbecue?*

   Repeat each line several times. Point out that the three sentences in each group should take about the same amount of time to say. For example, **Who** was at **Jenn**ifer's **bar**becue? takes no more time to say than **Where's Dave's lunch**? – there are more syllables in the first, but they are squashed between the stressed syllables.

   Optional: Use *Audio 1.12-1* to hear all of the lines in **Blocks 1-5**.

2. Repeat **Step 1**, but this time clapping a rhythm of four beats:

	clap	clap	clap	clap
You:	*a*	*a*	*a*	
	clap	clap	clap	clap
Students:	*Where's*	*Dave's*	*lunch?*	

   The stressed syllables in each of the students' words should fall on the beat which is marked by the clap. The fourth clap is a silence.

3. Repeat **Step 2**, but now mix up the sentences, e.g.:

	clap	clap	clap	clap
You:	*c*	*a*	*b*	
	clap	clap	clap	clap
Students:	*Who was at*	*Dave's*	*party?*	

4. Repeat the drill with the other blocks on the sheet, or get volunteers from the class to take the teacher's role and give letter combinations for their classmates to 'translate'.

1.12 Goes well with …

... **PronPack 4.18** for a lesson on rhythm.

1	a ●	**Where's**	**Dave's**	**lunch**?
	b ●●	**Where** was	**Mart**a's	**par**ty?
	c ●●●	**Who** was at	**Jenn**ifer's	**bar**becue?

2	a ●	**Eat**	**more**	**fruit**!
	b ●●	**Give** me	**lots** of	**app**les!
	c ●●●	**Buy** yourself	**plenty** of	**or**anges!

3	a ●	**Why**	**miss**	**Spain**?
	b ●●	**Won't** you	**vis**it	**Turk**ey?
	c ●●●	**Why** did you	**trav**el to	**It**aly?

4	a ●	**Two**	**wet**	**socks**.
	b ●●	**Lots** of	**coats** and	**jack**ets.
	c ●●●	**Hund**reds of	**box**es of	**sun**glasses.

5	a ●	**Ring**	**Jack**	**now**!
	b ●●	**Speak** to	**Al**ex	**lat**er!
	c ●●●	**Tel**ephone	**Car**oline	**af**terwards!

6	a ●	**Ten**	**young**	**kids**.
	b ●●	**Crowds** of	**nois**y	**child**ren.
	c ●●●	**Bus**loads of	**par**ents and	**teen**agers.

Tonic Stress Workout

focus on the person 😊:
She can swim.

focus on ➕ or ➖:
She **can** swim.

She can swim.

😊😊	➕/➖
Jim	was
I	don't
Anne	won't
They	were
Alice	is
Chris	has

TEACHING FOCUS
To raise awareness of tonic stress

MINIMUM LEVEL
Pre-intermediate

ACTIVITY
Choral chant/drill

WORKSHEETS
PronPack Worksheet 1.13
Print one copy for each student

AUDIO FILES

Background

Speech can divided into **tone units**, much as written text is divided into sentences. In each tone unit, one syllable is given the strongest stress – this is known as **tonic stress**.

Normally, tonic stress falls on the last content word in the tone unit. For example, in *Tom can swim*, tonic stress would normally fall on **swim**. However, a speaker may choose to place tonic stress on any word. For example, we may stress **Tom** to contrast with some other person mentioned in the conversation, or we may stress **can** to contrast with *can't* in a previous sentence such as *Tom can't swim*.

If tonic stress is not used in the same way in your students' own language they may be 'stress deaf' – that is, they may find it difficult to perceive or produce stress. This activity is intended to help them overcome this problem.

Presentation

1. Give out *Worksheet 1.13* and ask students to look at **Simple Statements**. Model the alternative pronunciations of *She can swim* as shown above the picture.

2. Explain that **Normal** means *without any special focus*. Explain that **Focus on the person** means that you want to give emphasis on the person, for example in answer to the question *who can swim?*. Explain that **Focus on + or -** means that you want to give emphasis on the to the positive or negative polarity of the auxiliary verb, for example in response to statement *She can't swim*.

3. Get students to try saying the sentences themselves.

Activity

1. Ask students to look at the chart in **Simple Statements**. Say sentences from the chart with one of the three words emphasised. Ask students to listen and say **A**, **B** or **normal**. For example:

   You: *Jim **was** here.*
   Students: *B!*
   You: *I don't **drive**.*
   Students: *Normal!*

2. Tell students to do the same activity in pairs or small groups. One of them says the sentences, the others identify which word is emphasised.

3. Ask students to look at **Wh- Questions**. Model the alternative pronunciations of *Where were you born?* as shown above the picture and get students to try saying the sentences themselves.

4. Explain that in **Wh- Questions** just as in **Simple Statements** we can focus on the person or the positive or negative. We can also focus on the question, for example: ***Where*** *were you born?* as opposed to ***When*** *were you born?*

5. Ask students to look at the chart in **Wh- Questions**. Say sentences from the chart with one of the four words emphasised. Ask students to listen and say *A*, *B*, *C* or *normal*. For example:

   You: *Where do **you** work?*
   Students: *C!*
   You: *Where **are** you staying?*
   Students: *B!*

6. Tell students to do the same activity in pairs or small groups. One of them says the sentences, the others identify which word is emphasised.

If you prefer, you can use *Audio 1.13-1* for both **Charts**.

1.13 Goes well with ...

... **PronPack 2.9**, **PronPack 3.10**, **3.11** and **3.12** for a lesson on tonic stress.

Normal :
She can **swim**.

Focus on the person 😊:
She can swim.

Focus on ➕ or ➖:
She **can** swim.

Simple statements

She can swim.

A 😊	B ➕/➖	Normal
Jim	was	here.
I	don't	drive.
Anne	won't	mind.
They	were	tired.
Alice	is	late.
Chris	has	gone.

Normal :
Where were you **born**?

Focus on the question ❓:
Where were you born?

Focus on ➕ or ➖:
Where **were** you born?

Focus on the person 😊:
Where were **you** born?

Wh- Questions

Where were you born?

A ❓	B ➕/➖	C 😊	Normal
Where	do	you	work?
Where	are	you	staying?
Why	did	they	leave?
What	will	we	do?
Where	does	she	live?
How	does	he	feel?
What	have	you	done?
How	can	I	help?

About the Author

Mark Hancock started teaching English over 30 years ago and wrote his first English language teaching book – *Pronunciation Games* – over 20 years ago. His approach in both teaching and writing ELT materials is to engage the learner and inspire their intrinsic interest in the content and in the process of the lesson. This is driven by his belief that teaching and learning a language can and should be an enjoyable experience.

He studied Geography and Philosophy at St. Andrews University, followed by teacher training courses and finally an MA in Teaching English from Aston University. Mark has taught in Sudan, Turkey, Brazil, Spain and currently lives and works in the UK. Apart from teaching and writing, he also presents at international conferences and leads on short teacher training courses.

In his free time, Mark plays the saxophone and guitar, paints in oils and walks in the mountains.

By the same author

ELT Pronunciation and Skills

- *Pronunciation Games* (CUP 1995)
- *English Pronunciation in Use Intermediate* (CUP 2003, 2012)
- *Authentic Listening Resource Pack* (Delta 2014 – co-authored with Annie McDonald)
- *Pen Pictures 1, 2 & 3* (OUP 1999 – 2000 – co-authored with Annie McDonald)
- *Oxford Advanced Learner's Dictionary 9th Ed 'Speaking Tutor' section* (OUP 2015)
- *Empower C1 'Everyday English' sections* (CUP 2016)
- *Singing Grammar* (CUP 1999)

ELT Course Book Series

- *English Result* (OUP 2007 – 2010 – co-authored with Annie McDonald)
- *Out and About* (CUP 2015 – co-authored with Annie McDonald)
- *Winners* (OUP 2010 – co-authored with Cathy Lawday)
- *New Ways to Go* (CUP 2002 – co-authored with Penny Ur and Ramon Ribé)

Acknowledgements

My first book, **Pronunciation Games**, was published back in 1995 by *CUP*. It was a photocopiable book of games with accompanying teachers' notes, designed by my sister Amanda Hancock. It seems appropriate that all these years later, my first ebooks **PronPack 1-4** should also be pronunciation activities – but printable rather than photocopiable this time – and again beautifully designed and produced by Amanda.

A huge thank you is also due to Annie McDonald for her editorial work and tireless encouragement, and to Henry Wong of Heliographic for his graphic design input.

I would also like to thank my students at *English in Chester* (www.english-in-chester.co.uk), who were the first to try out the activities in this book, and colleagues at that school who also trialled the material, especially Patsy Tyrer.

Last but not least I would like to thank my team of consultants/reviewers around the globe, including:

Freya Barua *(India)*
Marina Cantarutti *(Argentina)*
Ariel Donnell-Clark *(UK)*
Cristina Gómez Martínez *(Spain)*
Ewa Grzelak *(Poland)*
Louise Guyett de Orozco *(Ireland)*
Oksana Hera *(Ukraine)*
Stella Maris Palavecino *(Argentina)*
José Mompean *(Spain)*
Lalitha Murthy *(India)*
Catarina Pontes *(Brazil)*
Jane Neill *(UK)*
Adam Scott *(UK)*
Elena Velikaya *(Russia)*

Editor: Annie McDonald
Book design: Amanda Hancock
Graphics: Heliographic
Illustration: Mark Hancock
Images: Shutterstock.com
Audio: Mark Hancock with Annie McDonald

For more information visit **www.pronpack.com**

Notes